NO BIG DEAL

by Anne Sibley O'Brien
✳
illustrated by
Anna Rich

Scott Foresman

Editorial Offices: Glenview, Illinois • New York, New York
Sales Offices: Reading, Massachusetts • Duluth, Georgia
Glenview, Illinois • Carrollton, Texas • Menlo Park, California

My name is Susanna. I came home to my family when I was just a baby. Of course I had a birth mother and a birth father. But I never knew them. I'm so glad my parents wanted to adopt me. They are the couple who have always been my mom and dad. And they always will be.

When I was younger I didn't think much about being adopted. I loved the story of how I was born and how I became their child. I could always ask questions. They always gave me the answers they knew. Being adopted was no big deal. It was just part of me.

But then I got into fourth grade, and something happened. That's when I started thinking about who I am and how I'm like or different from other people.

My friends were wondering about some things too. All of a sudden I was getting all these questions.

One day my friend Chris asked me, "Do you remember your mother?"

I looked at him. I felt confused. What did he mean? He knew who my mother was.

That afternoon, I threw my atlas and my math book on the table. I asked my mom, "Who's my real mother?"

She smiled at me and asked back, "Who do you think?"

"Well, I think you are," I said. "I mean, you're the one who always takes care of me and everything."

"I think so too," my mom said. "Your birth mother and birth father are the couple who gave you life. That's a precious gift. But your dad and I are your parents. We're the ones who are raising you."

"Right," I said. I liked her answer.

A few days later, Chris asked me, "Do you know where your father is?"

"Yeah," I said right away. "He's at the hardware store, where he is every day."

But I was getting a funny feeling in my stomach. Chris looked confused. But he didn't ask me any more questions.

The next day at lunch, I saw Chris talking with Sarah. At recess, Sarah came up to me. She asked me the same questions that Chris had asked.

All of a sudden there was a lump in my throat. I was afraid I would start crying in front of Sarah, so I just walked away. I felt so sad. How come no one knew who I really was?

Later that day we shared the vocabulary project we'd been working on. We were making words for the letters in people's names. I showed the one I'd done for Maria.

Musical
Artist
Runs fast
Interesting
Awfully nice

Stephen had done mine. He began reading, "Smart. Unique. . . ." I froze when I heard the word *unique*. That meant different. I didn't want to be unique. I just wanted to be like everyone else. Mrs. Webster asked if I was okay. I told her nothing was wrong.

11

I had orchestra rehearsal after school. I didn't see my parents until supper.

"What's wrong, Muffin?" my dad asked. That was one of his funny pet names for me, but I didn't smile. I just sat with my head down, playing with my food. This was amazing because it was one of my favorites, rice and beans.

My mom said, "Were there more adoption
questions at school today, Susanna?" Then the
tears started spilling over. They landed, drip,
drip, on my plate.

"Oh, sweetheart," my dad said. He scooped
me up in a big hug. I cried for a long time.
Then my dad kissed me. "Now how about a
new plate of rice and beans?" he said. I giggled
and nodded.

The next day I didn't want to go to school.
My mom decided it was time to do something.

Later that week she came into my class. She
let the kids ask all the questions they wanted.
And she gave them lots of information. She told
them about adopting a baby.

My mom explained that when a couple chooses to adopt a child, they are a family forever. Then I got to tell them the parts of my story that I wanted to share. We even got out the atlas. It showed just where I was born. The kids really listened, and it felt kind of cool.

Things are better at school now. These days, I figure adoption is no big deal. It's just part of who I am. It's just one of the things that make me unique.

I'm UNIQUE
Mom and Dad
♥
Susanna
school
rice and beans
I love soccer
Drawing ✿